FIND YOUR
MONEY

How to Search for Unclaimed Funds

EDWIN HAYES

xulon
PRESS

To my dear Wife Sheila who since 1984 have seen the making of this book come together. Thank you for prayers and patience with me.

My children, who made me think dads can fix anything.

To my grandchildren, who know Grandparents can fix anything, with prayer.

Thank you heavenly Father for never leaving me nor forsaken me.

WHAT ARE UNCLAIMED FUNDS?

Each year, millions of dollars in assets are turned over to the State treasurers' offices in the form of cash, stocks, bonds, insurance benefits and even valuables from safe deposit boxes. State treasuries serve as custodians of these assets and make every effort to return them to the rightful owners or their heirs.

Unclaimed property laws have been around since at least the 1930s but have become much broader and more enforced in the last 15 years. Unclaimed property is one of the original consumer protection programs.

Every U.S. state; the District of Columbia; Puerto Rico; the U.S. Virgin Islands and Quebec, British Columbia and Alberta in Canada have unclaimed property programs that actively find owners of lost and forgotten assets.

WHAT'S IN A NAME

When you began a search, the last name is required. Money that was reported using incorrect spelling of an individual name or address, would have been returned to the reporting source.

The process may take several weeks or months to correct. When the reporting source receive any undeliverable funds, they are require to turn it over to State.

You may have moved however your money will remain in an account until you are located.

The way the reporting source listed your name may have revealed why it was not delivered to you in the first place.

Try variation of your last name if your name can be easily misspelled such as, Green or Greene. Do the same for first names. James may be listed as Jim and Robert as Bob or Rob.

Common last names such as Smith, Jones, or Hernández, may need more details, try adding first and middle name.

When searching for females account, remember to use maiden and married names. Their name may be listed by the biological parent name. This is also possible for siblings or adopted children.

Obituaries, old newspaper clippings, and tombstones will reveal names, dates, relatives, timeline of valuable information that can be used later.

Business cards list addresses of companies you or your family member, may have owned or had a position in. The company name maybe listed as a claimant.

Accounts may have more than one name, a husband and wife, siblings or Grandparents etc.

Finding unclaimed assets in your name is wonderful, yet you may find owners of funds belonging to your relatives or a friend of yours.

The unclaimed Property laws have been around since the 1930s. So there is a possibility that even your Great-Grandparents may have assets held by the State Treasurer department.

NATION OF TRAVELERS

—⁓∾∾⁓—

This nation is full of opportunities, seeking them out is the pride that drives us. New jobs, colleges, military assignments, marriage, relocation benefits, are just a few reasons why we move around.

Starting with your birthplace write down all States you have lived, (no matter how brief), if you worked out of state, list them also.

Military duty stations and their cities will lead to more detail work. Obtain a copy of your military records, payroll deductions to off post financial institutions.

Colleges and out-of-state training programs that you attend are States you can access to research for unclaimed assets.

Follow all the States you have worked in, remember to include the headquarters of the company, (money may be returned to the headquarters of a branch office).

Records of payroll deductions to financial institutions, old checkbooks, investments, stocks and insurance company payment ledgers will yield a wealth of information.

BUILD A SEARCH PLAN

—◦◦◦◦—

P lace the States in order, starting with the earliest to the present. Keep the information with the person you are researching together with that State.

The copies of information you've gather will aid you in building timelines for verification of rightful ownership.

Deceased relatives that you are heir to their estate, should be treated as you are searching for yourself.

A death certificate is issued in the county of death. You will need to establish the death of a claimant and your validation to the claim. Family lawyers, Probate orders and of course, last will and testimony.

FINDERS LOCATORS AND INVESTIGATORS

There are many businesses, sometimes called finders or locators, which find legitimate lost property for owners and offer to inform them of how to obtain it for a fee, usually a percentage of the total.

Ultimately the finder will ask you to sign a contract. The majority of firms that provide these services work within the law, but there are also many unclaimed property scams across the United States.

Before signing any contract from a firm of this type, we recommend that you be cautious and contact the unclaimed funds office in your state for more information.

www.unclaimed.org

The National Association of Unclaimed Property Administrators (NAUPA) is the primary starting point of State treasurers offices database design to linked with all States having unclaimed funds departments.

First select the State, a link to the Office or state Treasurer will appear. Some States require you to use an image verification process to prove you're a person typing in a search.

Next enter the name you are researching. Use the information previously discussed to help narrow the results.

The results displayed will give you many areas to consider;

Did you ever lived at the last known address city or State.

The reporting source, did you have any connection with them? If so you may be the rightful owner should consider submitting a claim inquiry.

Some States list the amounts in holdings, others will show an account indicating more or less than < > $100 dollars.

In some States you will see an entry of a few cents, because some people will not pursue filing for the claim, they miss out on the chance of a lifetime.

If you see a $0 dollars amount, this may mean that the funds need to be converted to cash before it can be released, i.e. safe deposit boxes, mineral rights, lands or artwork.

Since it is impossible to store and maintain all of the contents that are turned over from safe deposit boxes, most states hold periodic auctions and hold the funds obtained from the sale of the items for the owner.

Some states also sell stocks and bonds and return the proceeds to the owner in the same manner.

OTHER SOURCES OF UNCLAIMED PROPERTY

VA Insurance Benefits
www.VA.gov

Unclaimed insurance funds are owed to certain current and former policyholders or their beneficiaries. The money is owed to individuals whom have been unable to locate in order to make payment.

This money represents death awards, dividend checks and premium refunds that were mailed to policyholders. These payments were returned to VA by the Post Office because they could not be delivered. VA holds this money until we can locate the policyholder.

The VA site contains a record of monies owed to individuals by name only (the original policyholder's name). You can search for debts owed to you or to a relative.

However, even if there is a record under the name that you enter, the money may actually belong to someone else with the same name.

Important Note: The unclaimed funds search does not include SGLI and VGLI policies for those in service from 1965 to the present. Please do not use this search feature if you are a SGLI or VGLI policyholder.

If you had an FHA insured mortgage, you may be eligible for a refund from HUD/FHA.

www.HUD.gov

Who may be eligible for an FHA refund or share?

Premium Refund: You may be eligible for a refund of a portion of the insurance premium if you:

- acquired your loan after September 1, 1983
- paid an up-front mortgage insurance premium at closing and
- did not default on your mortgage payments.

Review your settlement papers or check with your mortgage company to determine if you paid an up-front premium.

Distributive Share: You may be eligible for a share of any excess earnings from the Mutual Mortgage Insurance Fund if you:

- originated your loan before September 1, 1983
- paid on your loan for more than seven years and
- had your FHA insurance terminated before November 5, 1990

DOCUMENTATION

━━ ᴄᴏᴄᴏ ━━

I f you find a result listed that you may be the claimant simply request a claim inquiry package.

Original or photo copies of documents of the following documents can help substantiate your right to the property;

- Birth Certificate
- Death certificate
- Driver license
- Social security card
- Marriage license
- Will or trusts

- Probate orders
- Insurance policies
- Power of Attorney
- Articles of incorporation
- Voters registration card
- Court documents showing appointment as personal representative

Affidavit of authority to receive and disbursement of funds for that person or company.

Tax return transcripts shows line items from your tax returns as it was originally filed, including any accompanying forms and schedules, available for the last 3 years, free.

RECORD EVERYTHING AND FOLLOW UP

K eep a record of when you started your search for funds.

The information you found.

The phone numbers, websites and emails

Dates and time of the day communication took place.

Most important the person you made contact with from beginning to end.

Complete, sign and return the claim inquiry package with as much of the requested identification you can provide.

States may be able to determine ownership based on the slightest information you are able to provide.

Allow 2-3 months for the States to review files and process your claim. Clams that involve minerals, stocks, estates or other complex issues may take longer.

Send your success stories to Edwin Hayes; Email address; ev7hayes@live.com

Thank you and may God's blessings overtake you.

OTHER SOURCES FOR UNCLAIMED PROPERTY

National Credit Union Administration
www.NCAA.gov

U.S. Federal Investments
www.treasuryhunt.gov

If you had an FHA insured mortgage, you may be eligible for a refund from HUD/FHA.
www.HUD.gov

Veterans Administration Benefits
www.benefits.VA,gov